# September 11th
# 2001

# From the Author

As a former Elementary School Teacher, a mother of four,
a grandmother of four and President of a publishing company,
I felt a real calling to write and publish a book about the events of
September 11th, 2001 for young children in the elementary school grades.

I have tried to keep the concepts simple yet be honest in portraying the
facts, stressing our patriotism over assault.

Copyright ©2002 Nancy M. Poffenberger

Cover illustration by Val Gottesman

Illustrations by: Students from Lotspeich School
(Cincinnati, Ohio)

International Copyright Secured Made in U.S.A.

All rights reserved. No part of this book may be used or reproduced
in any manner whatsoever without written permission except in the
case of brief quotations embodied in critical articles and review.

ISBN 0-938293-12-5

FREEPORT MEMORIAL LIBRARY

# Tuesday, September 11th, 2001

is a day many of us will remember well.

If you lived in New York City, Washington, D.C.
or the state of Pennsylvania
you certainly will never forget that day.

# Let's Begin with New York City

Close to 9 in the morning, when people were coming to work, an airplane flew right into one of the two towers of a place called the World Trade Center.

When people saw this on TV, they thought the pilot of the plane hit the building by mistake.

5

# A Short While Later

another airplane hit into the other tower.

When the second hit happened, the United States realized some group or groups were trying to hurt and scare us.

The name of the people who do this are called "Terrorists".

After both towers got hit, the buildings crumbled to the ground and thousands of people died.

After this, the same thing happened to a building called the Pentagon in Washington, D.C.

This building houses the Department of Defense.

People also died there.

# That Same Day

a fourth plane went down in an area of the State of Pennsylvania. It is believed this plane was also headed for Washington, D.C.

We learned that there were some very brave people on that plane who were able to stop "the Terrorists" from flying the plane into another building in Washington, D.C.

Cell phone calls helped the passengers learn what already had happened with the other planes, so they decided to go after "the Terrorists" on that plane.

The plane crashed in a field in Pennsylvania, but the people on the plane prevented "the Terrorists" from hurting any more people in Washington, D.C.

# We Learned That These "Terrorists"

who did this horrible act are groups of people around the world who do not like the way we live or the freedoms we have.

They do not like the idea that we have many religions in America.

They also think we are too rich and that we have too strong a military.

These people want to take over the world.

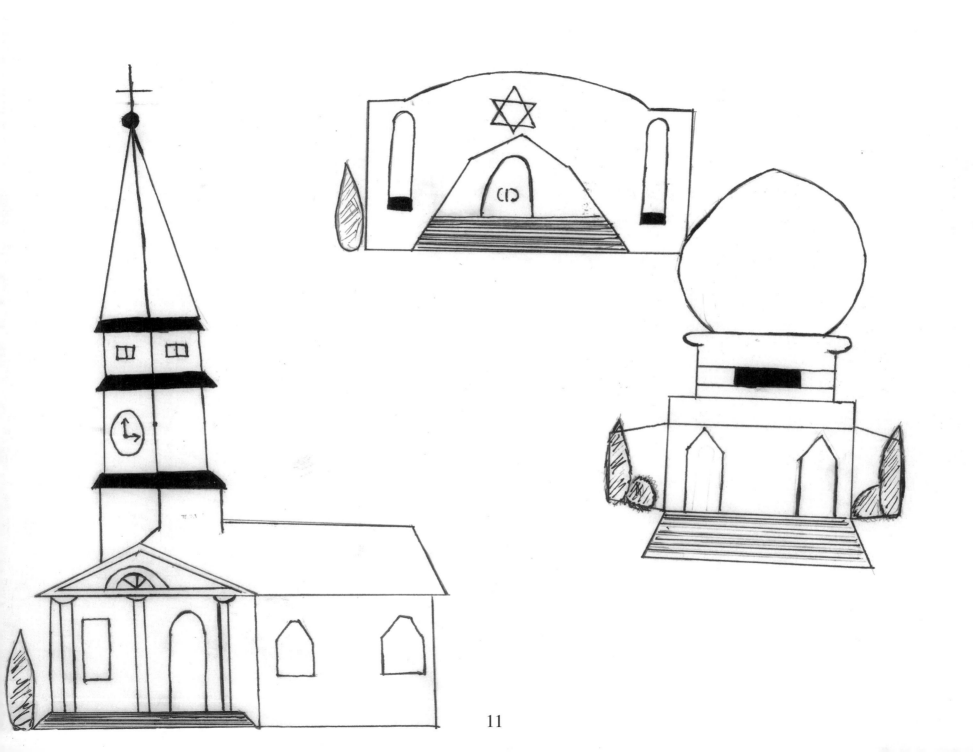

11

# People From All Over The Country & World

wanted to help the people in New York and Washington, D.C.

Firefighters, police and many other specialists came to
New York City.

Mayor Guiliani of New York City and Governor Pataki
were always there to help the city and its people.

President Bush also was a fine leader at this time.

The firefighters, police and emergency workers worked
day after day trying to find people who got hurt and
were under the collapsed buildings.

Parents and children helped collect money to send water
and food for the helpers who worked day after day.

Some people gave blood to those who had gotten hurt.

13

# People All Over The Country

became patriotic and wanted to show how much they loved our country.

Many homes and businesses put up a flag,

People sang songs such as 'God Bless America' and went to special church services all over the world.

Children and adults had lemonade stands, bake sales and donated money to groups who helped people in need.

# The People in the United States

all pulled together and stopped arguing over politics.

The leaders joined together with many nations
all over the world to form a coalition.

All of these nations became committed to fight "terrorism".

These people, who came together, wanted to show that life
would get back to normal, that they would again fly in planes
and that they would no longer be afraid of "the Terrorists".

The people of the United States wanted to say they love and
appreciate the freedoms they have here and that they are lucky
to be able to make the many choices they do each day.

# September 11th, 2001

## (a simple account for children)

Written by: Nancy Poffenberger

Cover illustration: Val Gottesman

Illustrations by students from
Lotspeich School

DISCARDED BY
FREEPORT
MEM'L LIBRARY

# Other Books by ~~Nancy~~ Poffenberger

FREEPORT MEMORIAL LIBRARY

3 1489 00476 7826

(who specializes in making things simple)

## instant "Piano Fun"™ Book One

The 1st in the key-tabbed method series. This has children's songs all done in ABC color-coded letters. For ages 4-7, Special Ed and young gifted children.

## instant "Piano Fun"™ Book Two

A second book in the key-tabbed method series. This one takes you through naturals, sharps, flat... reading.

## instant "Pia... Rhymes

Contains picture titles for ...kers on the keyboard to be m... ok.

## instant ...stmas

Features 18 fun Chris... ard, and the bells. Includes...Up On the House... and It's A Small World.

## instant "Recor... nd Book Two

Recorder Fun Book One all d... for a Montessori class... Book Two all do... ring chart... books co... rder.

A book written for Chr... old time favorites.

## Fun ... ne

All done in ABC's...w... note xylophone.

ASK YOUR LOCAL ... OTHER BOOKS

• Stained ☐

• Water Damage ☐

• Written In/Marked Up ☐

• Other (give details) ☒

_Check for loose Laminated Sheet_

**Levittown Public Library
1 Bluegrass Lane
Levittown, NY 11756
516-731-5728**

FUN PUBLISHING
2121 Alpine Place, Cincinnati, OH 45206

513-533-3636 • Fax: 513-421-7269

www.funpublishing.com

e-mail: funpublish@aol.com

# Author

Nancy was an elementary school teacher who graduated from Northwestern University where she was chosen "Outstanding Student Teacher".

She has written 10 teach-yourself music books plus educational booklets for other companies and runs her own Fun Publishing Co.

She is nationally known for her ability to simplify concepts and she felt a real need to do just that regarding September 11th, 2001.

Nancy does workshops and speaking with her teach-yourself music books.

ISBN 0938293

9 780938 293